HOW TO CARVE FACES IN DRIFTWOOD

by

Harold L. Enlow

Copyright © 1978 by Harold L. Enlow
Library of Congress Card Number: 78-53753
THIRD PRINTING

Printed in the United States of America

Typesetting and Layout by:
A B C Publishing Services, Inc.
1320-A North Stewart
Springfield, Missouri 65802

Printed by:
Western Printing Co., Inc.
665 Harrison
Republic, Missouri 65738

"Contents"

Foreword

Seems as if almost everyone has at one time or another had the urge to carve or whittle. You may have done nothing more than carve your initials on a "Sweetheart Tree". If you would like to further your carving skills, you may want to try driftwood faces.

The following projects were designed to give step-by-step instructions for carving facial features. They do not take much time to carve and the wood is usually free. If you ruin a few, just grab up a new piece of wood and start over.

By the time you have completed all the projects, you should be able to carve your own style of driftwood faces, and use the techniques you have learned for carving the faces on figures as well.

Harold L. Enlow
P. O. Box 18
Dogpatch, Arkansas 72648

FIG. 1. "Sweetheart Tree" in Buffalo National Forest, at Lost Valley, Ponca, Arkansas.

"Hunting Your Wood"

FIG. 2. A day's find on the lake.

Driftwood is an excellent source of wood for carvers. Not only is it free, but it makes some beautiful, one-of-a-kind, original carvings. Driftwood will be easier to find in some parts of the country than in others. If you live near the ocean, driftwood should be readily available for your use. In the Ozarks area, we are only an hours drive from several lakes.

If driftwood is not easily obtained in your area, you may use any suitable weathered wood which you can find. Often you can find excellent pieces along creeks and rivers, or in the woods. Old fence posts with a few staples and a strand or two of wire entwined make unique carvings. You may find usable pieces of wood in brush piles. Old house and barn timbers lend themselves well to carving. Hunting and finding unusual pieces of driftwood or weathered wood to carve is half the fun.

You will probably find yourself bringing home many pieces of wood which you cannot possibly use. After hunting for awhile, you will gain a certain amount of experience and will find yourself bringing home the more usable pieces.

Be sure the pieces of wood you choose are solid. Look from the bottom to be sure there are no holes or large cracks which will ruin your carving. Small surface cracks will enhance your carving, making it look more aged and rustic. You will also need an area large enough on which to carve your design. The kind of wood is important too. I prefer walnut, red cedar, osage orange, oak (occasionally), and American smokewood. Other times, you may find woods which carve well, but be uncertain of the kind. After awhile, you will be able to tell your favorite kinds of wood from a distance. It is wise to take along your pocketknife to make a small cut in an inconspicuous place on some of the unknown woods. You can usually tell the kind this way and also if it will carve well. A small chain saw or a handsaw can be used if you need to cut up a larger piece of driftwood or just want a certain part of a large piece.

In our lakes area, we have found that renting a boat is the best way to hunt for good pieces of driftwood (Fig. 2). This enables you to go to the remote coves of the lake where the driftwood washes in. It also eliminates carrying loads of wood for long distances. Wintertime is the best season for us to hunt driftwood. There are no snakes or ticks to be seen and most of the campers and fishermen are gone for the season. Sometimes the campers and fishermen burn the driftwood in their campfires. This accounts for some pieces having a black charred layer before you cut deeper into the piece, revealing the true color. This charred layer isn't always noticeable until you carve into it, because often the piece will drift again, rubbing most of the charcoal off, then turning gray once more. Some of the charred pieces give a better effect to the finished piece of work than do those with just one color. Usually the outside layer of most driftwood pieces will be case hardened and needs to be cut away where the carved design is to be. The first ¼ inch of the outer layer is usually the hardened part.

It is advisable to wear long sleeves and gloves when

hunting driftwood along the lake. You run into many bramble bushes. Also, be alert for ants, scorpions, spiders, and other insects when picking up the pieces of wood.

Nothing is more refreshing than to spend a day by the lake hunting driftwood. You may want to take along a picnic lunch.

"Sharpening"

After you have found your driftwood, you will want to be sure your tools are in good carving condition. While sharpening is always important to wood carving, it is especially true when carving on driftwood. All driftwood has sand and grit embedded in it which will dull your tools. You will find yourself sharpening more often when carving driftwood. Occasionally, you will hit small rocks or even pieces of metal or wire.

To keep your tools in shape, you will need a few materials which I have listed. You may use whatever substitutes you have as long as they will work for you.

1. India stone, 1″ x 2″ x 8″, medium or fine grit.
2. Arkansas slipstone, #42, for honing inside v-tools.
3. 2″ x 12″ piece of cowhide glued smooth side up onto a piece of wood.
4. Small jar of honing compound.
5. Kerosene or other light oil for use on the stones.

After you have glued the cowhide onto a piece of wood, one edge may be shaped with a sharp knife so the inside of a v-tool may be stropped. The other edge may be shaped to fit the inside of a small gouge. Some of the wood may be trimmed away from the block if necessary. A small leather wedge, cut to shape, may be used inside the v-tools if desired. You may prefer to use a buffing wheel fixed onto an electric motor or grinder instead of the cowhide and honing compound. It is easier to carry the leather and honing compound in your tool box. To use the buffing wheel, just turn on the motor and push a stick of polishing compound into the wheel so it will load up good. Once the wheel is loaded, use it to buff the bevels of your tools. This is the last step in sharpening and your tools must still be sharpened on some kind of stone first. The cakes of polishing compound may be purchased at industrial supply stores. The buffing wheel used for this procedure should be well sewn together, as a loose type doesn't work very well.

"KNIFE"

To sharpen your knife, first apply some kerosene to your India stone. Lay the knife blade flat on the stone,

then raise the back just slightly. Now the blade may be pushed and pulled while applying moderate pressure. After a few strokes, turn the blade over and push and pull equally on the other side. Keep repeating this sharpening procedure until the edge becomes sharp (Fig. 3).

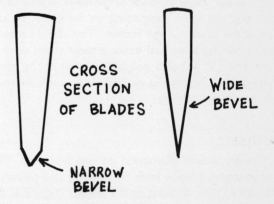

FIG. 3. Sharpening a knife on the stone.

When knives are new, some are sharp on the very edge. Usually the bevels are so short that they do not cut properly (Fig. 4). By laying the blade of your knife

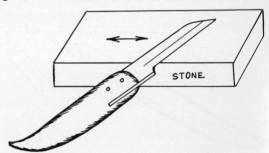

FIG. 4. Shows a narrow bevel on a new knife and how it looks when widened.

almost flat on the stone while sharpening, you are widening the bevel so the blade will slide through the wood easier (Fig. 5).

After you have widened the bevel, and the edge feels sharp, a little burr will usually form along the edge of the blade. This burr is a good indication that you are

3

almost finished with the sharpening process. To remove this burr, raise the back of the knife blade slightly higher off the stone and push lightly across the stone, first on one side, then the other. A few strokes on the stone will remove most of the burr. You will complete the process with your leather (Fig. 6). If you will apply your honing compound to your leather the

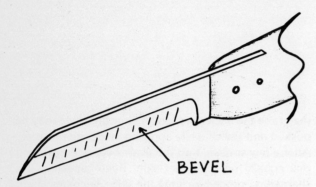

FIG. 5. *Bevel formed on a knife blade.*

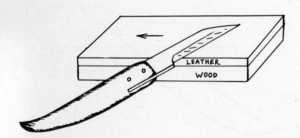

FIG. 6. *Stropping the knife on the leather.*

day before use, it will have time to dry out and will cut much better. Hold the back of the blade slightly higher than you did when sharpening on the stone. Be sure to pull the blade on the leather. This should remove the remaining burrs and make a razor sharp edge on your knife. It will also polish the bevel of the blade, cutting down on friction as it passes through the wood when you are carving.

"CHISEL"

I prefer chisels sharpened on one side only. They are sharpened like a knife by pushing and pulling on the stone, then stroking on the leather (Figs. 7 & 8). I sharpen only on the beveled side, then turn it over and stroke once or twice on the opposite side to remove the burr, holding the blade almost flat. If you prefer a wider bevel on your chisel as I do, you may want to widen it while sharpening. If you are going to carve strictly on very hard woods, you may prefer a narrow bevel on your tools. The wide, thin bevel works well for carving soft woods but may be easily broken when carving hard woods.

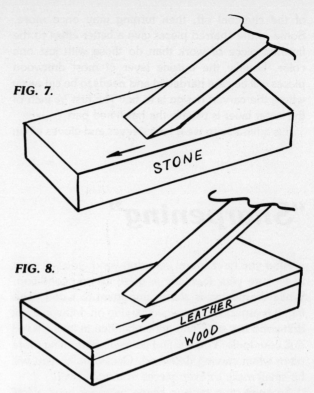

FIG. 7.

FIG. 8.

FIGS. 7 & 8. *Sharpening a chisel on a stone and leather.*

"GOUGES"

Gouges must be rotated from side to side while you are pushing and pulling on the stone so the edge will be sharp all around (Fig. 9). The burr on large gouges may be removed on one edge of your stone (Fig. 10).

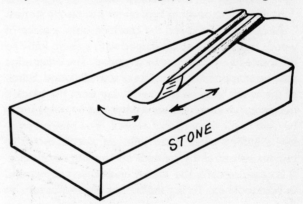

FIG. 9. *Sharpening a gouge on the stone.*

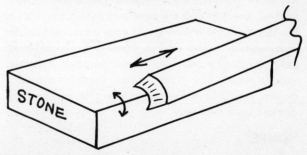

FIG. 10. *Burr being removed from a gouge on the edge of a stone.*

4

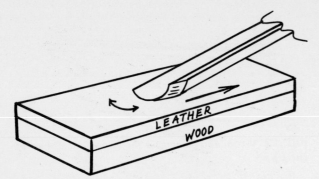

FIG. 11. Stropping the gouge on leather.

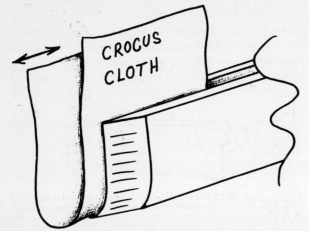

FIG. 12. Using crocus cloth to remove burrs from inside tiny gouges.

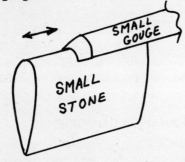

FIG. 13. Burrs being removed with a shaped stone.

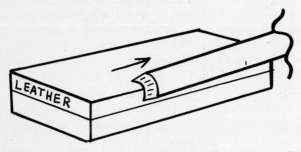

FIG. 14. Removing the burr inside a gouge by stropping.

A gouge must also be stropped on the leather (Fig. 11). Very deep and small gouges need the burr removed inside with crocus cloth or a small slipstone (Figs. 12 & 13). Use the edge of your leather or the leather wedge for stropping inside the other gouges (Fig. 14).

"V-TOOLS"

Sharpen each side of your v-tool as you would a chisel (Fig. 15). Next, round off the outside of the point on the stone (Fig. 16). Most v-tools are slightly rounded inside at the point. Rounding off on the outside makes it conform to the way it is ground inside, leaving you with a sharp, slightly rounded point. Strop

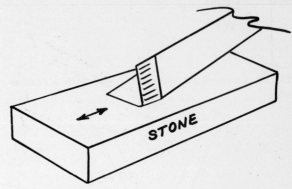

FIG. 15. V-tool being sharpened on the stone.

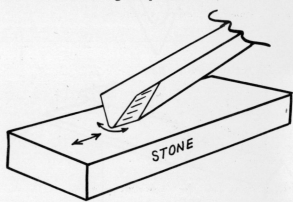

FIG. 16. Rounding off the outside of a v-tool.

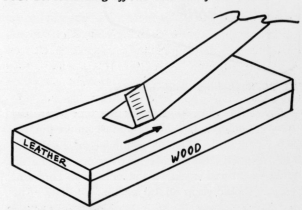

FIG. 17. Stropping the outside of the v-tool on leather.

the outside bevels and outside the point on your leather (Fig. 17). Strop the inside, using the leather cut to shape (Fig. 18).

The v-tool is the problem tool for many people. After sharpening, if your tool does not cut well or tears the wood, something is wrong. Usually it is ground slightly wrong inside (Fig. 19). To remedy this, some metal has to be ground away inside (Fig. 20). You will

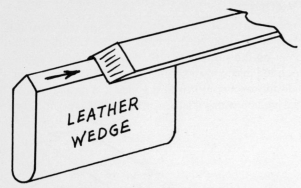

FIG. 18. *Stropping inside the v-tool with a leather wedge.*

FIG. 19. *A v-tool with a flaw.*

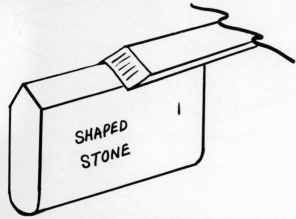

FIG. 20. *Reshaping inside a v-tool.*

actually be beveling some inside the tool where the arrow is pointing in Fig. 21. You must square the tool again at the end, either on a grinder or sharpening stone. Sharpen the outside all over again. The tip should be ground again on the outside to conform, then you should strop on the leather.

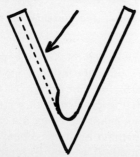

FIG. 21. *Shows where metal should be beveled on a v-tool with a flaw.*

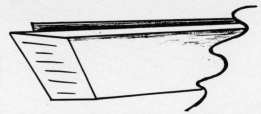

FIG. 22. *V-tool sharpened so the edges cut ahead of the tip.*

Fig. 22 shows a v-tool that has been sharpened so the edges cut ahead of the tip. This style of sharpening works well except for corners. Fig. 23 shows a tool sharpened so it will cut well into corners, but doesn't cut well otherwise as the tip cuts first. A v-tool which is 90 degrees or squared across the end before it is sharpened works well for all types of cuts.

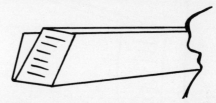

FIG. 23. *V-tool sharpened with the tip cutting ahead of the edges.*

Sometimes a v-tool will have more than one flaw inside, or one side may be thicker than the other. Whatever you find wrong, you can remedy by sharpening some inside and some outside. You may need to look closely under a magnifying glass or bright light to find the smallest problems. With a little patience and practice, you can become a real expert at v-tool sharpening.

"SMALL U-SHAPED GOUGES"

Small u-shaped gouges are sharpened like regular larger gouges, except they may have the same problems as a v-tool. Some may be ground slightly wrong inside. You will have to make adjustments and sharpen some inside and some outside. A common flaw in tiny u-shapes is a square corner on the inside, usually on one side and sometimes on both sides (Fig. 24). The inside has to be ground with sandpaper wrapped around a small piece of wood or a slipstone shaped to fit. To correct the flaw shown in the figure, sharpen away metal inside to the dotted line.

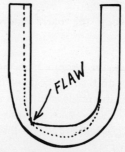

FIG. 24. *Flaw in a small u-shaped gouge.*

6

"Preparing and Holding the Wood"

Put your driftwood in a place where it can dry thoroughly. Use a stiff brush to remove all the sand and dirt from the surface.

A simple holder may be made in which to hold your driftwood piece while carving. If you try to place the piece in a vise without attaching it to a holder, you will have dents and scratches on your finished carving. The holder (Fig. 25) is made from a scrap piece of board, preferably a hardwood such as oak. Most of the time, I use a holding board about 18 inches long and clamp the board in the vise. If you have no vise, use a holding board 2 or 3 feet long and clamp the ends to the carving bench with c-clamps.

Screws hold the piece of driftwood snugly on the holding board. The back of the piece of driftwood must be flattened enough so it will be tight against the board. Large pieces are flattened with a chain saw and small pieces on the bandsaw. You may use various other means to flatten the backs such as a hatchet, handsaw, or other hand tools. Some pieces of driftwood may be sawed down the center, giving you two pieces to carve and flattening the backs at the same time.

Small pieces of driftwood may be carved without a holder, by just holding them in your lap, and using small hand tools.

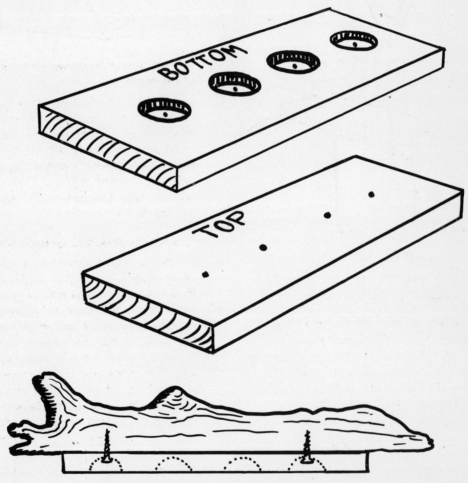

FIG. 25. A holder for carving driftwood.

"North Wind"

FIG. 26. Pattern for "North Wind".

TOOLS USED:
MALLET
50-MILLIMETER SHALLOW GOUGE
10-MILLIMETER V-TOOL
12-MILLIMETER CHISEL
16-MILLIMETER SHALLOW GOUGE
10-MILLIMETER DEEP GOUGE
8 -MILLIMETER DEEP GOUGE
3 -MILLIMETER MEDIUM GOUGE
6 -MILLIMETER V-TOOL
8 -MILLIMETER SKEW
KNIFE

Since the North Wind is to be a windy fellow (Fig. 26), you will want his cheeks puffed out as if he is blowing with all his might. This face was carved from a piece of walnut driftwood, but you may use any suitable type driftwood or other weathered wood. If you prefer, you may even use a piece of a log or other wood of your choice. Since the carving of faces seems to give people the most trouble, carving these faces in driftwood is excellent practice for facial details.

If you are using driftwood, it will be easier since the carving area will be slightly rounded already. Carving of these driftwood faces will be almost like relief carving. Remember, your piece of wood may not exactly fit the pattern as no two pieces are ever identical. Improvise as needed. Often, a particular piece of wood will suggest changes which can be made to add interest to the carving. Perhaps you will want to add more hair to some of the patterns if your wood allows. Whiskers and hair seem to add lots of character to driftwood carvings.

After you have chosen your wood, cleaned it as well as possible, and flattened the back, you are ready to transfer your pattern. First, trace the pattern onto a piece of tracing paper by laying it over the pattern. Attach your wood to a driftwood holder and clamp with c-clamps or hold in the vise.

I am listing the tools which I have used. Use tools of your preference. These are tools which are easiest for me, but you may substitute by using a similar tool which works best for you. A knife may be used in many places if you do not have the correct tool. Tools will save you time. With few exceptions, you will use basically the same tools for each project. The type of wood may determine tools to use in some instances.

Except for the finest details, the mallet will be used almost exclusively. Although I will not specify use of the mallet with each tool, it should be used and will save you much time and energy.

FIG. 27. Use a 50-millimeter shallow gouge or large

FIGS. 27 to 37. Step-by-step instructions for carving "North Wind".

FIG. 27.

chisel and a mallet to carve off an area large enough for you to draw on your design. Place carbon paper under the pattern and trace the design onto your wood. Masking tape may be used to hold the pattern and carbon paper in place. If your design does not show up well, go over it with a black marker or a black grease pencil.

FIG. 28.

FIG. 28. Use a 10-millimeter v-tool and mallet to outline the design. Use a 12-millimeter chisel to set in along the top of the head, under the chin, and on the sides. Setting in is usually done with a chisel, but you can use various shapes of gouges or a knife. To set in, just drive your chisel in along the outline of your design. I usually hold the chisel with the beveled side of the blade away from the design. After you have set in all or part of your design, you must cut some wood away from the background, called wasting away. Carve towards the chisel cuts, using gouges. For this project, a 16-millimeter shallow gouge will be used for wasting away the wood from the background of the areas which you have set in. This will leave the head and face raised. The complete background will not be carved, just enough so the face is standing out, or as desired to complement your piece of wood. The depth you carve will depend upon your particular piece of wood and its thickness. This background was carved to a depth of approximately 1 inch near the head, then tapering out and blending into the background. An 8-millimeter skew will be helpful for cutting wood

FIG. 29. FIG. 30. FIG. 31.

FIG. 32.

FIG. 33.

away around the tips of the hair. The neck of the carving will blend into the background.

FIG. 29. Use a 10-millimeter deep gouge to carve away wood across the bridge of the nose, approximately ¼ inch deep, and along the side of the nose. Carve the eye sockets in ¼ inch deeper than the bridge of the nose. By using a gouge to carve out these areas, your cuts will be more gradual, blending the cheeks and the sides of the nose together. Carve wood away under the nose a little deeper than you did on the bridge.

FIG. 30. As you are carving, some of the lines of your design will be cut away. Draw or trace them back on where needed. Using the 10-millimeter v-tool, outline the cheeks, next to the hair, cutting away a little of the hair outside the cheeks. This will keep you from losing the lines of the cheeks.

FIG. 31. Next, carve away from the mouth and cheek area, leaving the nose the highest point on the face. Use the 50-millimeter shallow gouge. Since his cheeks are puffed out, do not remove much wood here. Start beneath the bottom lip and taper off the chin.

FIG. 32. Round the top of the head, still using the 50-millimeter shallow gouge. Start halfway down on the forehead and round over the top to the background. Round the cheeks out near the edges.

FIG. 33. Outline the hair and the tops of the eyebrows with the v-tool. Cut away wood about 1/8 inch on the forehead between the areas which you have outlined, leaving the eyebrows and hair higher than the forehead.

10

FIG. 34.

FIG. 35.

FIG. 36.

FIG. 34. Cut straight in beneath the nose with a chisel or shallow gouge, making the cut more definite. With the 10-millimeter deep gouge, carve on each side where the cheeks and mouth meet, going from the nose down towards the chin. This will separate the cheek and mouth area. With an 8-millimeter deep gouge, carve deeper at the inside and outside corners of the eye sockets, leaving a mound for the eye in the center.

FIG. 35. Round and shape the nose, using the 12-millimeter chisel and your knife as needed. Carve the nostrils with a 3-millimeter medium gouge. Finish rounding the cheeks and shape the chin and mouth area. Draw on the lines for the eyes.

FIG. 36. Use the 6-millimeter v-tool to carve the eyes. Carve a groove underneath the eye line, forming a bag beneath the eye. Carve another line above the eye line, forming the eyelid. Deepen the eye cut with your knife so it will cast a greater shadow than the other grooves. Carve a groove across for the mouth, separating the lips. Use the 3-millimeter medium gouge to carve a hole in the center between the lips. Use your knife and chisel to further shape the lips. Carve the indentation under the nose. A 6-millimeter v-tool was used to carve the wrinkles in his forehead and above his nose. Use the same tool to carve the hair and eyebrows. Carve the grooves showing the neck lines. Shape and blend these lines into the background. The carving should now be completed. I do not sand my driftwood carvings, but again, this is a matter of preference. If your cuts are not nice and clean, you may want to sand off any burrs.

FIG. 37. Finishing driftwood is easy. I applied a coat of tung oil to the carved area only. Buff when dry for a soft hand-rubbed finish. The tung oil enriches the natural beauty of the walnut wood. The area outside your carving should have a nice gray patina which will need no finish if you are using driftwood. For hanging, nail a sawtooth hanger to the backs of small driftwood pieces. You will need to use screw eyes and picture hanging wire for large driftwood carvings.

FIG. 37.

"Inventor"

FIG. 38. Pattern for the "Inventor".

TOOLS USED:
50-MILLIMETER SHALLOW GOUGE
10-MILLIMETER V-TOOL
10-MILLIMETER DEEP GOUGE
16-MILLIMETER SHALLOW GOUGE
12-MILLIMETER CHISEL

6 -MILLIMETER V-TOOL
3 -MILLIMETER V-TOOL
5 -MILLIMETER SHALLOW GOUGE
3 -MILLIMETER DEEP GOUGE
KNIFE

Yellow cedar driftwood was used for carving the Inventor (Fig. 38). Trace your pattern as previously described. Flatten the back of your driftwood and clamp the piece in your holder. Smooth the area which will be carved, using a 50-millimeter shallow gouge. Transfer your pattern to the wood.

FIGS. 39 to 52. Step-by-step instructions for carving the "Inventor".

FIG. 39.

FIG. 39. Using your 10-millimeter v-tool, start at the tip of the mustache on one side and outline along the side of the face, across the top of the forehead, and down the other side of the face to the tip of the mustache on that side. Cut across the width of the face, crossing the bridge of the nose beneath the eyebrows with a 10-millimeter deep gouge. Gouge out this area about ½ inch in depth.

FIG. 40. A 16-millimeter shallow gouge will be used to recess the complete forehead area. Taper the hair on the sides coming into this forehead area. The hair around the top of the head will not be tapered as much as the sides.

FIG. 41. Starting at the eyebrows, set in down both sides of the face to the tips of the mustache with a 12-millimeter chisel. Use the 16-millimeter shallow gouge to waste wood away from the cuts which you have set in, again starting at the eyebrows. Most of the lower hair lines will be cut away. You will be cutting fairly deep in these areas, so you may have to set in again and repeat the wasting away process. Taper the hair in towards the face. Actually, when you are finished, the hair along the sides will be recessed behind the face. Your cuts will be about 1 inch deep right at the cheek area.

FIG. 42. Cut across under the nose as you did across the bridge of the nose. This cut will be approximately ½ inch deep. If you will use a 10-millimeter deep gouge for this crossgrain carving, you will have smoother cuts. A shallow gouge may dig in and tear the wood.

FIG. 40.

FIG. 41.

FIG. 42.

14

FIG. 43.

FIG. 44.

FIG. 45.

FIG. 43. Use the 10-millimeter gouge to carve wood away from both sides of the nose.

FIG. 44. Complete the preliminary carving of the chin area with a 16-millimeter shallow gouge. The chin, mustache, mouth, and whiskers need to be carved the same depth as the cheeks. Draw the lines back on which have been cut away.

FIG. 45. Outline the mounds for the eyes with a 6-millimeter v-tool. Deepen the inside and outside

FIG. 47.

FIG. 46.

corners of the eyes with your knife. The nose will have a hump of wood remaining which needs to be cut away and tapered towards the bridge.

FIG. 46. Outline the eyebrows and the glasses with a 3-millimeter v-tool. Carve away wood on the forehead all around the glasses and eyebrows to a depth of 1/16 inch. The glasses and brows will stand slightly higher than the forehead. Use a 5-millimeter shallow gouge for carving the forehead area. A chisel and knife may be needed to clean out the difficult areas. To carve the rims on the glasses, make a small v-groove around the inside of the rims. Recess the lenses slightly deeper than the rims, using a chisel and knife as needed.

FIG. 47. Outline the large locks of hair and the mustache with a 10-millimeter v-tool.

FIG. 48.

FIG. 49.

FIG. 50.

FIG. 48. Shape and round the nose and cheeks with a 12-millimeter chisel. Smooth as much as you think necessary. Some woods will require more smoothing than others, depending upon the type which you are carving. After shaping the cheeks, use a 10-millimeter deep gouge to carve a sunken area beneath the cheekbone. Carve and shape the mustache. Cut some wood away beneath the chin with a 12-millimeter chisel.

FIG. 49. Carve detail on the hair, eyebrows, and mustache with the 6-millimeter v-tool. Next, round and shape the chin with the chisel. Use a small gouge to carve a groove under the bottom lip. Round the chin into this groove. Cut a small groove between the bottom lip and mustache, forming his mouth. Your knife may be used for this cut which will be small and show only slightly.

FIG. 50. Draw the eyes on as they are shown in the pattern. Carve the grooves in the eyes with a small v-tool, carving just inside the lines which you have drawn on. Deepen these cuts with your knife tip. Fig. 50 shows one eye partially carved.

16

FIG. 51.

FIG. 51. Recess and shape the eyeball with your knife. Draw the iris and pupil onto the eyeball. Use a 3-millimeter gouge and push straight in, forming the pupil of the eye. Do not remove the pupil, just push the gouge in to form an outline. Next, push a 6-millimeter gouge in to form the iris. Use a tiny gouge or your knife to carve out the iris. This will create a shadow which will look like a real eye from a distance. Both eyes will be carved the same.

FIG. 52. A coat of shellac will bring out the color in the yellow cedar. After the shellac is thoroughly dry, apply a coat of paste floor wax. Buff with a brush when dry.

FIG. 52.

FIG. 53. Pattern for the "Tree Troll".

FIG. 55.

FIG. 56.

FIG. 54.

TOOLS USED:
MALLET
50-MILLIMETER SHALLOW GOUGE
10-MILLIMETER DEEP GOUGE
8 -MILLIMETER DEEP GOUGE
8 -MILLIMETER SHALLOW GOUGE
12-MILLIMETER CHISEL
6 -MILLIMETER MEDIUM GOUGE
6 -MILLIMETER V-TOOL
KNIFE

A section of an old red cedar fence post was used to carve the Tree Troll (Fig. 53). Prepare the wood for carving as you did in the two previous projects. Since wood preparation will be exactly the same for the remaining projects, I will eliminate this part of the instructions. If in doubt, refer back to project #1.

FIG. 54. Make a cut all the way across the face beneath the nose, using the 10-millimeter deep gouge. This cut will be ½ inch in depth. A similar cut will be made across the top of the face, crossing the bridge of the nose. The bridge of the nose will be about ¼ inch deep. Gouge out wood where the eye sockets will be, making them deeper than the bridge of the nose.

FIG. 55. Use the 10-millimeter deep gouge to carve wood away from the sides of the nose. Starting about 2 inches below the nose, carve wood away from the chin and mouth area, using the 50-millimeter shallow gouge. Taper from the chin area, leaving the nose the highest point on the face.

FIG. 56. Outline the bottom of the leaves and the top of the eyebrows with the 10-millimeter v-tool. Carve the wood on the forehead (between the leaves and the eyebrows) about 1/8 inch deep. Taper the top of the nose, blending it into the bridge.

FIGS. 54 to 64. Step-by-step instructions for carving the "Tree Troll".

FIG. 57. Draw the lines back on which have been carved away. Use the 10-millimeter deep gouge to make deep cuts at the corners of the mouth and outline the under parts of the cheeks with an 8-millimeter deep gouge. The cuts at the corner of the mouth will be 3/8 inch deep. Use an 8-millimeter shallow gouge to smooth the mouth area.

FIG. 57.

FIG. 58.

FIG. 59.

FIG. 60.

FIG. 58. Outline the tops of the leaves and the outside of the face with the 10-millimeter v-tool. Carve a little wood away from the tops of the leaves, leaving them higher than the background. Cuts along the sides of the face will be 3/8 inch deep.

FIG. 59. Finish outlining the leaves with the v-tool. Outline the whiskers, forming locks of hair. Again, use the v-tool for the hair and whiskers. No wood will be carved away beneath the beard, but the whiskers will blend into the background. Draw any hair back on which has been carved away. Outline and carve locks of hair which will also blend into the background.

FIG. 60. Use your knife and 12-millimeter chisel to round the cheeks, sides of the face, and around the mouth area. Since the Tree Troll is smiling, his cheeks should be nice and round. Make a horizontal cut across the face, just below the bottom lip, with the 8-millimeter deep gouge. Round and shape the nose, using your chisel and knife where needed. Carve the inside and outside of the nostrils with a 6-millimeter medium gouge.

FIG. 61. Draw the mouth back on and carve the mouth line with a 6-millimeter v-tool. Deepen the mouth cut with your knife tip so it will cast a good shadow. Round the bottom lip slightly. Shape under the bottom lip, over near the sides, with your knife. Blend the whiskers into the chin area with the 10-millimeter gouge. Some of the leaves will be behind other leaves as you can see from the pattern. Use a 12-millimeter chisel to flatten and slightly recess the leaves which are behind others. Also, flatten and smooth the top leaves.

FIG. 61.

FIG. 62.

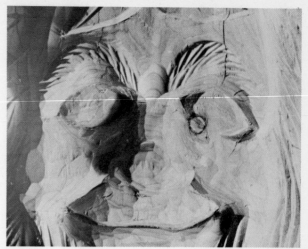

FIG. 63.

FIG. 64.

FIG. 62. Draw the veins on the leaves and carve with a v-tool. Carve the eyebrows, beard, and hair with the v-tool also. Some locks of hair and whiskers will be more prominent than others. Do not carve the hair and beard all one depth, but be sure to carve the locks on different planes. This will create shadows, giving your carving more artistic appeal.

FIG. 63. Carving eyes is often a trouble spot for beginning carvers. With practice, you will learn a few basic cuts for carving eyes with different expressions. To carve these eyes, use a 6-millimeter v-tool to cut deeper at the inside and outside corners of the eyes. Make a v-cut across the top and bottom of the eye sockets, forming mounds for the eyes. The figure shows the right mound completed and the left eye corners only deepened.

FIG. 64. Complete the mound on the left eye. Draw the lines on the eyes and carve with a small v-tool. Deepen these v-cuts with your knife tip. The crow's feet at the corners of his eyes and the wrinkle in his forehead are also carved with the v-tool. Finish with shellac and wax.

"Prophet"

FIG. 65. Pattern for the "Prophet".

TOOLS USED:
MALLET
50-MILLIMETER SHALLOW GOUGE
10-MILLIMETER V-TOOL
10-MILLIMETER DEEP GOUGE
8 -MILLIMETER DEEP GOUGE
8 -MILLIMETER SHALLOW GOUGE
12-MILLIMETER CHISEL
6 -MILLIMETER MEDIUM GOUGE
3 -MILLIMETER V-TOOL
KNIFE

FIGS. 66 to 73. Step-by-step instructions for carving the "Prophet".

FIG. 66.   FIG. 67.

FIG. 68.

The Prophet (Fig. 65) was carved from a piece of cedar driftwood. It is charred along the bottom edge. If a piece is charred too much, you may want to wire brush part of the burned area away. Sometimes a charred area can be worked into part of the piece. Although each project has a different face, you will probably begin to notice that many of the instructions are basically the same. Learning these basic instructions and repeating them will help you carve almost any type of face with ease.

FIG. 66. First, outline the right side of the Prophet's face with a 10-millimeter v-tool. A 10-millimeter gouge will be used to carve away some of the background around the right side of the face. Carve this background area 1 inch deep if your piece of wood allows. Outline the top of the hair with the v-tool. Remove some wood from the background around the top of the hair. Cut approximately ¼ inch deep here.

FIG. 67. Make a horizontal cut, ½ inch in depth, across the face beneath the nose, using the 10-millimeter deep gouge. Carve across the face at the bridge of the nose, taking care not to carve into the eyebrows. The bridge of the nose will be about ¼ inch in depth. Carve deeper for the eye sockets, making them about 3/8 inch deep.

FIG. 68. Use a 10-millimeter deep gouge to carve wood from the sides of the nose. Outline the tops of the eyebrows and the hairline with the v-tool. Remove wood from the forehead with an 8-millimeter shallow gouge. The forehead will be about 1/8 inch deeper than the hair and eyebrows.

FIG. 69. Although the chin will be covered with the whiskers, you will need to carve wood away from the

chin and mouth area, blending into the groove at the base of the nose. Your 10-millimeter deep gouge may be used for this step. Carve the locks in the hair and beard with the v-tool. The locks will be carved the same as they were in the previous project. Again, the beard will blend into the background.

FIG. 69.

FIG. 70.

FIG. 71.

FIG. 72.

FIG. 70. Draw on the mouth and mustache. Use the 10-millimeter deep gouge to scoop out wood for the mouth. Use a smaller gouge to deepen the mouth, making it about ½ inch in depth. Next, outline the mustache with the v-tool. Cut a groove beneath the bottom lip with an 8-millimeter deep gouge. Start approximately 1 inch below the bottom lip and taper the whiskers into the groove beneath the lip, using the 8-millimeter shallow gouge.

FIG. 71. Shape the nose with your chisel and knife. Carve the inside and outside nostrils with the 6-millimeter medium gouge. Hair, eyebrows, and whiskers will be carved with the v-tool.

FIG. 72. Shape and smooth the cheeks and face area. Carve the cheeks so they have a sunken look beneath the cheekbone. Use the 8-millimeter shallow gouge. Wrinkles in the forehead can be carved with a 3-millimeter v-tool. To carve the eye sockets, use a 10-millimeter v-tool to carve deeper at the inside and outside corners of the eyes. Use a 3-millimeter v-tool to deepen these cuts. Carve lines above and below the eye sockets, forming mounds on which to carve the eyes. Carve the crow's feet at the outside corners of the eyes with the small v-tool.

FIG. 73. Since these eyes are also closed, draw a line across the mounds and carve with a small v-tool. Deepen the cuts with your knife tip. Shellac the carving, then apply a light stain (burnt umber acrylic, thinned with water) to the hair, beard, mustache, and eyebrows. Let dry, then wax with paste floor wax and buff with a brush. This is another simple finishing technique which looks very good on driftwood carvings.

FIG. 73.

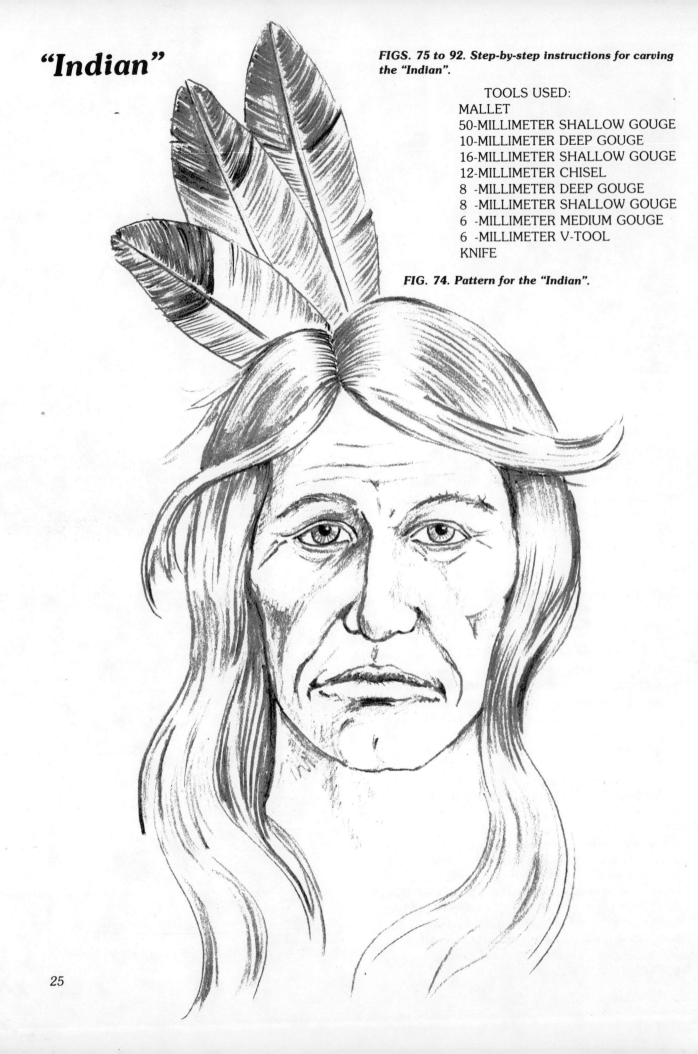

"Indian"

FIGS. 75 to 92. Step-by-step instructions for carving the "Indian".

TOOLS USED:
MALLET
50-MILLIMETER SHALLOW GOUGE
10-MILLIMETER DEEP GOUGE
16-MILLIMETER SHALLOW GOUGE
12-MILLIMETER CHISEL
8 -MILLIMETER DEEP GOUGE
8 -MILLIMETER SHALLOW GOUGE
6 -MILLIMETER MEDIUM GOUGE
6 -MILLIMETER V-TOOL
KNIFE

FIG. 74. Pattern for the "Indian".

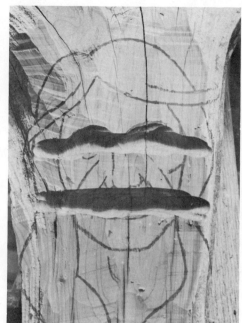

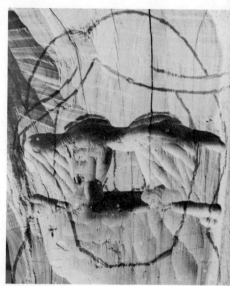

FIG. 77.

FIG. 75.

FIG. 76.

FIG. 78.

FIG. 79.

You will notice that the Indian I have carved will vary slightly from the pattern (Fig. 74). Some of these changes were made to accommodate the piece of red cedar driftwood. My piece of wood has an area which suggests a natural feather, so I will adjust the feathers to make use of this wood. The hair will be changed somewhat along the sides because this piece of wood isn't as wide in back as it is in front. Variations caused by the wood will make your carvings more original even if you have used a pattern. Work with the wood whenever possible. If the wood suggests something to you, try it. Soon your driftwood pieces will be as individual as you are.

FIG. 75. Trace your pattern onto the wood. You may leave the feathers off and draw them on later.

FIG. 76. Cut across the bridge of the nose with the 10-millimeter deep gouge, cutting about ¼ inch in depth. Make the horizontal cut beneath the nose also, cutting about ½ inch deep.

FIG. 77. Draw the sides of the face back on where the lines have been cut away. Carve wood away from both sides of the nose, still using the 10-millimeter deep gouge. Keep drawing your lines back on the face as they are cut away, so you will not lose the lines.

FIG. 78. Sketch a line across the face at the bottom of the chin, extending beyond the face area to the sides of your wood. These will be guide lines for later positioning of the chin. Use the 16-millimeter shallow gouge, start at the neck area, and carve wood from the entire lower face, carving the same depth as the base of the nose. Draw on the chin, being sure to use the lines you have drawn on for correct positioning.

FIG. 79. Use the 10-millimeter v-tool to outline the hair above the forehead and along the top of the head. Also, outline the face.

26

FIG. 80.

FIG. 81.

FIG. 82.

FIG. 83.

FIG. 80. Carve the forehead area, including the eyebrows, to a depth of approximately 1/8 inch. A 16-millimeter shallow gouge and a 12-millimeter chisel can be used to smooth the forehead. Set in with the 12-millimeter chisel all around the face. Waste wood away from the area which you have set in, using the 16-millimeter shallow gouge. You may need to repeat the setting in and wasting away process several times to get the depth you need. Background wood at the temples will be cut to a depth of 3/8 inch. Again, the depth will depend upon your piece of wood. Draw hair back on which has been cut away.

FIG. 81. Set in along the top of the head. Waste wood away from the top of the head as you did on the sides. Set in again and repeat until the background right around the top of the head is recessed to a depth of 5/8 inch.

FIG. 82. Use the v-tool to outline the neck. Carve and shape the neck and upper chest area, being sure the chest is cut in deeper than the surrounding hair. Use the 16-millimeter shallow gouge and an 8-millimeter shallow gouge for carving the chest and neck. Outline the two locks of hair just above his forehead. Use a chisel to round and shape the top of his head (above the locks of hair) over to the background. Carve the part in his hair with the v-tool.

FIG. 83. Taper the hump of the nose back towards the bridge with the 12-millimeter chisel. Round and shape the face. Cut the grooves extending from the outside nostrils down towards the jaw line with the 10-millimeter deep gouge. Use an 8-millimeter deep gouge to cut deeper at the outside edges of the nostrils. A 50-millimeter shallow gouge will be used to cut wood away from the chin. Start just below the bottom lip and angle down towards the neck, leaving the mouth area higher than the chin. The tip of the chin should be only ¼ inch higher than the neck.

FIG. 84.

FIG. 85.

FIG. 86.

FIG. 84. Shape the nose, being careful to blend the areas where the nose and cheeks meet so you will not have a sharp line in this area. Use the chisel, 8-millimeter deep gouge, and knife as needed. Carve the inside of the nostrils with a 6-millimeter medium gouge. Using a 10-millimeter deep gouge, carve wood away from the outside of the eye sockets toward the edge of the face, making the cheekbones more prominent. Next, shape the mouth by blending outward towards the grooves which you carved running from the nostrils towards the jaw. Use a 12-millimeter chisel. This shaping should leave the center of the lips the highest point in this area. Be sure to shape this area before carving on the mouth. Otherwise, the mouth of your Indian will be flat.

FIG. 85. A chisel will be used to carve wood away from the temples, leaving the cheekbones the widest part of the face. As you are carving the temples, go ahead and shape the forehead. Using a 10-millimeter deep gouge, start up near the inside corner of the eye sockets and carve a groove downward, running parallel to the groove which you carved from the nose down to the jaw. Sketch on the mouth. Use a chisel to cut down toward the chin beneath the bottom lip. Cut upward from the chin towards this cut, forming a groove which separates the lips from the chin. Carve the mouth with a 6-millimeter v-tool. Start at the center of the mouth and carve out to one edge of the

mouth. Start at the center again and carve out to the other edge of the mouth. Use a 10-millimeter deep gouge to make a cut on each side of the chin. Carve the mounds in the eye sockets by deepening the corners with a 6-millimeter v-tool. Make a cut over and under the sockets, forming the mounds. Carve a little wood from the cheek areas, beneath the eyes.

FIG. 86. Using the 16-millimeter shallow gouge, start near the front of the cheeks and cut a small amount of wood from the sides of the face beneath the cheekbones. This will also help make the cheekbones more prominent. The area between the two parallel lines (running from the nose to the jaw) may be a little high. If so, you should carve some of the wood away to lower them slightly. Complete shaping of the lips, using a chisel, 8-millimeter deep gouge, and your knife. Carve the indentation under the center of the nose. Round, shape, and smooth the chin.

FIG. 87. Carve the lower locks of hair with an 8-millimeter deep gouge. Use a 6-millimeter v-tool to finish carving grooves in for the hair, including the hair above the forehead.

FIG. 88. Next, draw on the feathers. As previously mentioned, the feathers on this carving have been changed to fit the piece of wood. First, outline the feathers with a 6-millimeter v-tool. Use the chisel to carve a little of the background from around the feathers. Draw the shafts on the feathers and outline with the v-tool. Carve the barbs of the feathers. Finish rounding and shaping the eye mounds.

FIG. 89. Carve on the eyebrows with a 6-millimeter v-tool. Draw on the eyes. Cut a groove across the top and bottom of the mounds.

FIG. 87.

FIG. 88.

FIG. 89.

29

FIG. 90.

FIG. 90. Use your knife to round, shape, and smooth the eyeballs between the grooves you have carved above and below. Draw on the irises and pupils.

FIG. 91. To carve the eyes, you will need to gouge out the iris in each eye. Use a gouge the size of the iris or smaller. Be careful not to break off the eyelid when carving out the iris. After the iris is carved, push a small gouge in to outline the pupil of the eye. The pupil was not carved out in this carving but outlined only. However, you may carve the pupil in deeper than the iris if desired.

FIG. 92. Shellac the carving. Stain the hair with an acrylic wash, using burnt umber mixed with water. Wax and buff.

FIG. 92.

FIG. 91.

"Disciple"

FIG. 93. Pattern for the "Disciple".

TOOLS USED:
MALLET
50-MILLIMETER SHALLOW GOUGE
16-MILLIMETER SHALLOW GOUGE
10-MILLIMETER DEEP GOUGE
10-MILLIMETER V-TOOL
12-MILLIMETER CHISEL
8 -MILLIMETER MEDIUM GOUGE
8 -MILLIMETER DEEP GOUGE
3 -MILLIMETER SHALLOW GOUGE
5 -MILLIMETER DEEP GOUGE
2 -MILLIMETER DEEP GOUGE
KNIFE

FIG. 95.

FIG. 96.

FIG. 94.

FIGS. 94 to 104. Step-by-step instructions for carving the "Disciple".

FIG. 94. The "Disciple" is carved from walnut drift-wood. Use a 10-millimeter deep gouge to cut across the face at the bridge of the nose. Since I am using a thick piece of wood, this carving will be carved in deep relief, having more depth than the previous projects. Carve the depth as your piece of wood allows. The bridge of the nose is carved ½ inch deep.

FIG. 95. Starting at the top of the head, use a 16-millimeter shallow gouge to cut away wood from the whole upper head area (above the eyes and bridge of the nose). Cut away about 3/8 inch of wood on the forehead and brows. Figure 95 shows half of this procedure completed.

FIG. 96. Draw the hair and brow back on the side which you have just finished carving. Carve the remaining side of the head and draw the lines back on as you did on the first side. Carve across the face beneath the nose to a depth of ¾ inch, using a 10-millimeter deep gouge.

FIG. 97. Use the deep gouge to carve wood away from the sides of the nose. Carve the eye sockets, sloping gradually from the brows.

FIG. 98. Draw the sides of the face back on. Starting halfway down on the beard, carve upward, removing most of the wood up to the groove beneath the nose. Use the 16-millimeter shallow gouge.

FIG. 99. Start at the part in the hair above the forehead and outline the face on each side with the 10-millimeter v-tool. Also, outline the top of the head. Draw on the mustache, mouth, and beard.

FIG. 97.

FIG. 98.

FIG. 99.

FIG. 100.   **FIG. 101.**   **FIG. 102.**

FIG. 100. Set in around the sides and top of the head with the 12-millimeter chisel. Waste wood away from the background around the area which you have set in, using the 16-millimeter shallow gouge. You may need to use a smaller gouge in difficult places for setting in and wasting away. Repeat the setting in and wasting away several times until your background is 5/8 inch deep at the top of the head and even deeper (approximately 1 inch) along the sides.

FIG. 101. Use the 16-millimeter gouge to carve the sides of the hair down until the hair is lower than the face. The hair should be 5/8 inch lower at the cheek and brow, tapering upward towards the top forehead and tapering downward towards the cheek. Outline the mustache with the 10-millimeter v-tool.

FIG. 102. Shape the forehead, using the 16-millimeter shallow gouge and a chisel as needed. Carve the hump off the nose with the 12-millimeter chisel, blending towards the bridge of the nose. Use the chisel to round off the top of the head and to shape the cheeks. Round and shape the mustache, using your chisel and knife.

FIG. 103. Shape the nose, again using the knife and chisel. Carve the inside and outside nostrils with an 8-millimeter medium gouge. Use the 8-millimeter deep gouge to carve a groove on the bottom part of the eye sockets, forming the mounds. Cut deeper at the inside and outside corners, but *do not* carve a groove above the eye sockets as the Disciple will have sleeping eyes. To carve a sleeping eye, you will blend from the eyebrow down to the bottom of the eye. Carve out the small mouth with a 3-millimeter shallow gouge. Outline the bottom lip with an 8-millimeter deep gouge. Carve a little wood from the chin area, blending up into the bottom lip. The 8-millimeter deep gouge will also be used to carve locks in the beard and hair. Since I am carving a long piece of wood, you will notice that I have lengthened the beard so that it is longer than shown in the original pattern. Blend the lower tips of the whiskers into the background. The deep gouge was used instead of the v-tool to show a different technique for carving hair. The gouge will give a softer look to the hair than the v-tool.

FIG. 103.

FIG. 104.

FIG. 104. Use a smaller gouge (5-millimeter deep) to further detail the hair, beard, and mustache. Carve some of the smaller grooves deeper to catch light and cast shadows. Carve the eyebrows, again using a gouge rather than a v-tool. A 2-millimeter deep gouge or similar size will work best for the eyebrows. A small v-tool will be used to carve a groove along the bottom edge of the eyelid. Deepen the cut with your knife tip. Use the v-tool to carve the wrinkles in the forehead. Finish your carving as desired.

"Forty-Niner"

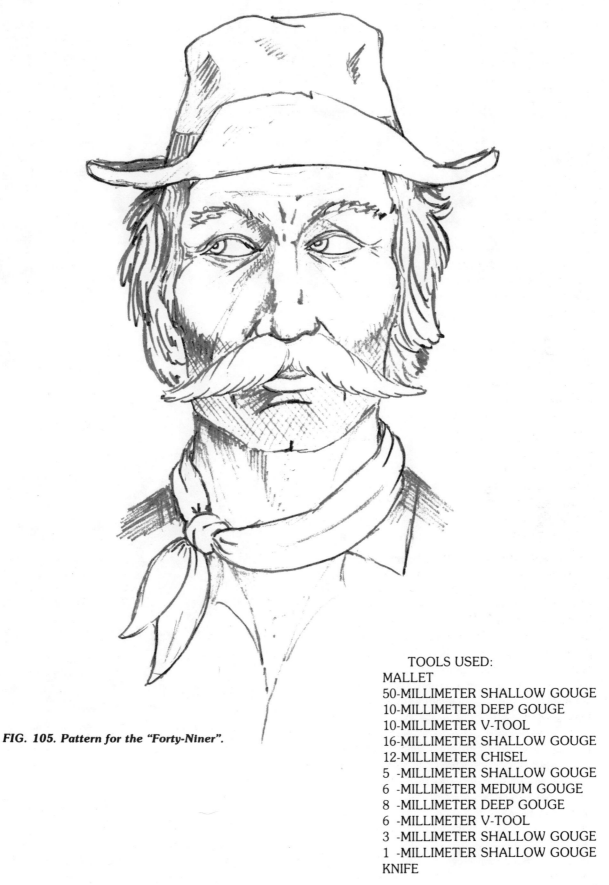

FIG. 105. Pattern for the "Forty-Niner".

TOOLS USED:
MALLET
50-MILLIMETER SHALLOW GOUGE
10-MILLIMETER DEEP GOUGE
10-MILLIMETER V-TOOL
16-MILLIMETER SHALLOW GOUGE
12-MILLIMETER CHISEL
5 -MILLIMETER SHALLOW GOUGE
6 -MILLIMETER MEDIUM GOUGE
8 -MILLIMETER DEEP GOUGE
6 -MILLIMETER V-TOOL
3 -MILLIMETER SHALLOW GOUGE
1 -MILLIMETER SHALLOW GOUGE
KNIFE

FIG. 106.   **FIG. 107.**   **FIG. 108.**

FIG. 109.

FIGS. 106 to 115. Step-by-step instructions for carving the "Forty-Niner".

FIG. 106. Again, I am using red cedar driftwood. Cut across the bridge of the nose to a depth of ¼ inch, using a 10-millimeter deep gouge. Also, cut across the face beneath the nose to a depth of approximately ½ inch. A v-tool will be used to carve a groove separating the hat from the forehead.

FIG. 107. Carve wood away from the sides of the nose with a 10-millimeter deep gouge. Draw the sides of the face back on. Outline the top of the hat and the top of the hat brim with a 10-millimeter v-tool.

FIG. 108. Starting at the bottom part of the shirt, carve upward towards the groove beneath the nose, using the 16-millimeter shallow gouge. You will be carving away the scarf, chin, mustache, and mouth lines. Carve the wood down to the same depth as the base of the nose. Draw all the lines back on which have been cut away. Use the chisel to lower the forehead to the depth of the groove at the bottom of the hat brim. Smooth the forehead and draw the sides of the forehead back on. Set in around the top of the hat and waste wood away from the background. A 12-millimeter chisel and a 16-millimeter gouge will be used for setting in and wasting away. Repeat, if necessary, until you have reached the desired depth of the background. Carve about ¾ inch deep at the top of the hat and ½ inch deep at the sides of the hat, just above the brim.

FIG. 109. Carve the hat (above the brim) 1/8 inch deeper than the brim, using the 12-millimeter chisel. Set in along the sides of the face and underneath the

hat brim. Also, set in beneath the mustache along the sides of the neck and the tops of the shoulders. Take care not to break off the tips of the mustache. Waste wood away from the background of the set in areas. The depth along the sides of the face will be about ½ inch. Carve ¾ inch deep along the sides of the neck and top of the shoulders.

FIG. 110.

FIG. 111.

FIG. 112.

FIG. 110. Draw on the hair at the sides of the head. Set in around the hair and waste wood away from the background. Repeat this procedure until the background around the hair is 3/8 inch deep. Blend the background areas around the hair into the background areas alongside the neck. Outline the chin with the 10-millimeter v-tool. Set in along the chin and remove wood from the neck and chest to a depth of 3/8 inch (right beneath the chin). Your cuts will become more shallow until they blend into the shirt and taper out into the background. The mustache will be outlined with a 10-millimeter v-tool. Round and shape the top of the hat, using a chisel and a 16-millimeter shallow gouge. The shallow gouge will be used to make cuts in the top of the hat, giving it a crumpled look.

FIG. 111. Use the chisel to carve some wood from the chin and mouth and from the cheeks, leaving the mustache higher. Draw on the neckerchief. Carve the hump off the nose. Round and shape the face on both sides, using a chisel. Chisels are excellent for rounding. The shaping and smoothing can be completed at the same time when using a chisel. Shape the nose. Carve the outside nostrils with a small shallow gouge (approximately 5-millimeter). Use your knife if needed. Carve the inside nostrils with a 6-millimeter medium gouge. Shape the hair.

FIG. 112. Gouge out the mouth with the 5-millimeter shallow gouge. Carve a groove beneath the mouth, separating the mouth and chin. Round and shape the chin, blending into the groove beneath the mouth. Outline the neckerchief with a v-tool. Carve and shape the neck, leaving the neckerchief standing higher. Use your chisel, 5-millimeter gouge, and knife as needed. Carve a little wood from below the neckerchief. Shape the neckerchief with the chisel and knife. The hair and mustache will be carved with a 6-millimeter v-tool. Again, you must carve carefully near the tips of the mustache so they will not be broken. Outline the neck of the shirt with a v-tool. Cut wood away on the chest area (beneath the neckerchief) so the shirt is higher. Carve wood from the shirt beneath the collar, leaving the collar higher.

FIG. 113.

FIG. 113. To carve the eyes, use the v-tool to first carve deeper at the inside and outside corners of the eye sockets. Next, carve a line above and below the sockets. The figure shows the right eye cuts made first with a v-tool, then smoothed and refined with the knife. The left eye shows cuts made with a v-tool only.

FIG. 114. Draw on lines for the eyelids. Use a small v-tool to carve the eyelids and the lines beneath the eyes. Round and shape the eyeballs between the two grooves, using your knife tip. The figure shows the right eyeball carved. The left eye shows only the grooves carved.

FIG. 114.

FIG. 115.

FIG. 115. After both eyeballs are shaped and smoothed, push in a 3-millimeter shallow gouge to outline the irises. Carve the irises in with a 1-millimeter shallow gouge. His eyes should be turned to the side, making him look somewhat suspicious. You will notice that eyes turned to one side or the other will look more alive, rather than having a blank, staring look. Push in the 1-millimeter shallow gouge to form the pupils of the eyes. Carve on the eyebrows, wrinkles in the forehead, and the crow's feet at the outside corners of the eyes with a small v-tool. Sink the cheeks in by carving away some wood beneath the cheekbone. For the whiskers, push the 3-millimeter v-tool slightly into the wood and quickly pop out tiny pieces. Keep these cuts close together. You may want to practice this technique on a scrap piece of wood until you can pop out the pieces easily. Put a few whiskers part of the way down on his neck and a few on his chest, if desired. Shellac the carving. Let dry, then stain the hair, eyebrows, mustache, and whiskers lightly, using burnt umber acrylic mixed with water. When dry, wax and buff.

"Hermit"

TOOLS USED:
MALLET
50-MILLIMETER SHALLOW GOUGE
10-MILLIMETER DEEP GOUGE
5 -MILLIMETER DEEP GOUGE
8 -MILLIMETER DEEP GOUGE
10-MILLIMETER V-TOOL
16-MILLIMETER SHALLOW GOUGE
8 -MILLIMETER SHALLOW GOUGE
4 -MILLIMETER DEEP GOUGE
6 -MILLIMETER V-TOOL
6 -MILLIMETER MEDIUM GOUGE
3 -MILLIMETER SHALLOW GOUGE
3 -MILLIMETER DEEP GOUGE
2 -MILLIMETER DEEP GOUGE
KNIFE

FIG. 116. Pattern for the "Hermit".

FIG. 117.

FIG. 118.

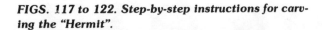

FIGS. 117 to 122. Step-by-step instructions for carving the "Hermit".

FIG. 116. A piece of mulberry firewood has been chosen for carving the "Hermit". This was trimmed off my mulberry tree about five years ago. The bark has rotted off, but the wood is still solid. Mulberry wood is hard and needs to be worked with large tools and a mallet. It will take detail quite well.

FIG. 117. Carve across the bridge of the nose to a depth of 3/8 inch with the 10-millimeter deep gouge. Carve across the face beneath the nose to a depth of 1/2 inch. Use the same gouge to carve wood from the sides of the nose.

FIG. 118. Use an 8-millimeter deep gouge to outline the top of the forehead where it meets the hair. Outline the tops of the eyebrows and remove wood from the forehead (between the tops of the brows and the hair). The brows will not be carved down on this project, but left at their original height so they will look big and bushy. Draw the left side of the face back on which has been carved away. Outline the left side of the face with a 10-millimeter v-tool and carve wood away from the background (on the hair area) with a 16-millimeter shallow gouge. Carve approximately ¾ inch deep at the cheek and forehead, getting shallower down near the mustache.

FIG. 119. You will notice from the pattern that the "Hermit" has his head turned to the left, rather than looking straight ahead. You will need to carve some wood from his left eyebrow, left side of his forehead, and the left side of his cheek. Use an 8-millimeter deep gouge and a 16-millimeter shallow gouge as needed.

FIG. 119.

After you have the left side of the face carved down, you will have carved and shaped almost down to the background. Carve the background down deeper if necessary, depending upon the amount of shaping you will have to do to make the face look in propor-

FIG. 120.

FIG. 121.

FIG. 122.

tion. After you have the left side of the face shaped, carve the hump off the nose. Round and shape the nose and carve the eye sockets, cutting deeper at the inside and outside corners of the eyes, forming the mounds. Carve the inside and outside nostrils with an 8-millimeter deep gouge. Refine the outside nostrils with an 8-millimeter shallow gouge. Outline the right side of the face.

FIG. 120. The eyes will be carved similar to the eyes in the "Forty-Niner" project. Carve grooves at the top and bottom of each eye mound, then remove wood between the grooves to form the eyeballs, using your knife. Another groove will be carved beneath the bottom of the eyes to form a bag. Push a 6-millimeter medium gouge in to outline the irises. Carve out the irises with a 3-millimeter shallow gouge. Carve in the pupils with a 3-millimeter deep gouge. Use a 4-millimeter deep gouge to carve on the eyebrows. Define the eyebrows by going over them with a 2-millimeter deep gouge. Carve wrinkles in the forehead with a 2-millimeter deep gouge, also.

FIG. 121. Draw the hair back on his left side. Use a 10-millimeter deep gouge to taper the chin and mouth area towards the base of the nose. Draw on the mouth, beard, and mustache. Outline the locks of hair, beard, and mustache with the 10-millimeter deep gouge. Carve on the mouth with a 3-millimeter shallow gouge. Use an 8-millimeter deep gouge to carve a groove beneath the mouth, forming the bottom lip. Blend the chin whiskers up into the groove beneath the bottom lip.

FIG. 122. Carve in beneath the cheeks with an 8-millimeter shallow gouge, to give them a sunken look. Details will be carved on the hair and whiskers with an 8-millimeter deep gouge. Go over some of these cuts with a 5-millimeter deep gouge, making deeper cuts which will cast shadows. Shellac and wax or finish as desired.

"Cigar Smoker" - Carving a Face Without a Pattern

FIG. 123. Pattern for the "Cigar Smoker".

TOOLS USED:
MALLET
50-MILLIMETER SHALLOW GOUGE
10-MILLIMETER DEEP GOUGE
8 -MILLIMETER DEEP GOUGE
16-MILLIMETER SHALLOW GOUGE
10-MILLIMETER V-TOOL
12-MILLIMETER CHISEL
6 -MILLIMETER V-TOOL
6 -MILLIMETER MEDIUM GOUGE
3 -MILLIMETER SHALLOW GOUGE
KNIFE

FIGS. 124 to 127. Step-by-step instructions for carving the "Cigar Smoker".

FIG. 124. I seldom use patterns for my work, especially when carving the driftwood pieces. If you will let the wood dictate what you carve, you will find it will turn out much better. I am going to carve this project, then draw the pattern to be used, if needed. The pieces seem to have a more relaxed look when carved without a pattern and can be carved much faster. Perhaps you will want to try one without using the pattern. This chapter is for those who might be interested in this procedure. The wood used is a piece of red cedar driftwood with a small limb sticking out which will make a perfect natural cigar. It is not too difficult to find a piece of wood of this type. Little extras like the natural cigar will make your carving more unique. However, if you cannot obtain a piece with a limb, just leave the cigar off and carve on a mouth. The cigar may also be carved separately and glued into the mouth. Smooth off the area to be carved, using the 50-millimeter shallow gouge. Place the driftwood in your holder. Cut across the face where the base of the nose is to be, using a 10-millimeter deep gouge. Also, cut across the bridge of the nose. You may want to draw on lines for placement of the features if you are unsure. Figure out where the hairline is to be and cut across here.

FIG. 125. Carve wood from the sides of the nose and carve in the eye sockets, using the 10-millimeter deep gouge. Recess the mouth area around the cigar (if your piece of wood has one). If you have no cigar, the mouth still needs to be recessed. Use the 50-millimeter shallow gouge to lower the forehead about 1/4 inch, leaving the nose and hair higher than the forehead.

FIG. 126. Use the 10-millimeter deep gouge to carve some locks of hair which will radiate from the

FIG. 124.

FIG. 125.

FIG. 126.

FIG. 127.

forehead. Carve a groove from the left side of the mouth over to the cigar and around the top and bottom of the cigar with a 10-millimeter v-tool. Reverse the procedure if you have a cigar on the left side rather than the right. Try to carve the cigar on one side or the other. It will look better than if it is in the middle of his mouth. Carve the hump off his nose and cut in a little deeper at the bridge. Use an 8-millimeter deep gouge to carve deeper at the inside and outside corners of the eyes, forming mounds. Carve a groove beneath the mouth, separating the lip and chin, using a 10-millimeter deep gouge. Starting at the corners of the mouth, carve a groove up to the outside of the nose with a 10-millimeter v-tool, separating the cheeks from the mouth. Use a 10-millimeter deep gouge to carve locks of hair, forming the beard.

FIG. 127. Starting just above the eyebrows, carve a groove across the forehead with the 10-millimeter deep gouge. This should leave the eyebrow area standing higher. Blend the forehead into this groove, using a 16-millimeter shallow gouge. Shape the nose with a 12-millimeter chisel, 16-millimeter shallow gouge, and knife. Outline the outside nostrils with a 6-millimeter v-tool. Carve the inside nostrils with a 6-millimeter medium gouge. Shape and smooth the mouth area with a 12-millimeter chisel. Shape the lips with the chisel and your knife. If you have a cigar, carve carefully around the base of the limb. You will need to take small cuts or tiny pieces of wood will chip out, going the wrong direction. Carve the groove under the septum.

Use a 6-millimeter v-tool to carve the grooves above the eye mounds, forming his eyelids. Carve a groove across the lower part of the mounds. Carve another groove above the eyelid. Start at the inside corners of the eyes and carve a groove downward on the cheeks. Carve from the outside corners of the eyes to the groove on the cheeks, forming bags beneath the eyes. Refer to figures for placement of these lines, if needed. Round the eyeballs as you have done in the previous projects, using your knife. Usually when you have eyes carved to this stage, one eye and eyebrow will be slightly higher than the other. We will carve his eyes turned in the direction which is the highest. This is another instance of the wood dictating how you will carve the piece. Use a 6-millimeter medium gouge to outline the irises. A 3-millimeter shallow gouge will be used to carve out the irises. Push a 3-millimeter deep gouge into the irises, forming the pupils.

Carve the sides of his face in, just below the cheekbones, so they will have a sunken look. Use the 16-millimeter shallow gouge. Carve on the eyebrows with the 6-millimeter v-tool. Carve hair and whiskers on the locks which you carved previously, again using your v-tool. Complete the carving with a finish of your choice.

42

"Carving a Feminine Face"

FIG. 128. Pattern for "Carving a Feminine Face".

FIG. 129. Shows differences in male and female bone structure.

FIG. 128. The girl will be carved from walnut driftwood or wood of your choice. Since a female face has smaller details than the facial features on the previous projects, I would recommend working slowly. Study the pattern and figures carefully. This will be the most difficult project in the book.

FIG. 129. While carving the profile on a female face, keep in mind the bone structure at the brows. The male has a heavier bone here than the female. Blend the forehead gently into the bridge of the nose so your carving will have a feminine look.

FIG. 130. Use the 10-millimeter deep gouge to carve across the bridge of the nose, carving deeper at the eye sockets. The bridge of the nose will be ¼ inch in depth. Carve wood from the sides of the nose on the cheeks. Carve a groove about 3/8 inch deep beneath the nose. Cut the mouth and chin area down to the same depth as the cheeks.

FIG. 130.

TOOLS USED:
MALLET
50-MILLIMETER SHALLOW GOUGE
10-MILLIMETER DEEP GOUGE
12-MILLIMETER CHISEL
16-MILLIMETER SHALLOW GOUGE
5 -MILLIMETER DEEP GOUGE
8 -MILLIMETER SHALLOW GOUGE
8 -MILLIMETER DEEP GOUGE
6 -MILLIMETER V-TOOL
1 or 2 -MILLIMETER V-TOOL
10-MILLIMETER MEDIUM GOUGE
5 -MILLIMETER MEDIUM GOUGE
4 -MILLIMETER DEEP GOUGE
2 -MILLIMETER DEEP GOUGE
5 -MILLIMETER DEEP GOUGE
KNIFE

FIGS. 130 to 135. Step-by-step instructions for "Carving a Feminine Face".

FIG. 131. Carve the forehead down (not quite as deep as the bridge of the nose), being sure to stay inside the hairlines. Carve the hump off the nose, dipping in slightly so the nose will have a turned-up look. Carve a little deeper at the bridge of the nose if necessary (until the nose looks correct to you).

FIG. 131.

FIG. 132.

FIG. 132. You will need to deepen the eye sockets again, using the 10-millimeter deep gouge. Draw the face back on, being careful to get the facial features in the exact places. This is very important when carving the female face. Use your ruler to take measurements from your pattern and transfer them to your wood. Use the 12-millimeter chisel to set in around the face. Waste wood away from the areas which you have set in, using the 10-millimeter deep gouge. You will be carving the wood away where the hair is drawn on along the sides and carving some of the neck area away beneath the chin. Repeat the setting in and wasting away until the background around the chin and face is 5/8 inch in depth. As carving progresses, you may have to cut the background even deeper as you are rounding and shaping the chin and face. Set in along the top of the head and waste wood away from the background.

FIG. 133. The 12-millimeter chisel will be used to round and shape the face and chin. A chisel is used as it will make smoother cuts than a gouge. There may be a few areas where you will need to use the 16-millimeter shallow gouge, but use the chisel whenever possible. Smooth and shape the forehead, remembering to blend the bridge of the nose and the forehead as shown in Fig. 129. The eyebrows will probably be carved out of position when you are shaping the forehead. If so, you will need to reposition them. Carve around the nostrils with a 5-millimeter deep gouge. Smooth around the mouth and nostrils with an 8-millimeter shallow gouge. Be sure to leave a mound on which to carve the mouth. Use the 8-millimeter deep gouge to carve deeper at the corners of the eyes, forming the eye mounds. Round off the top of the head with the 16-millimeter shallow gouge.

FIG. 134. Draw on the mouth. Use the chisel or knife to carve down from the top lip and up from the bottom lip, forming the groove between the lips. Shape and refine the lips with the knife. The top lip will stick out a little farther than the bottom lip. I have turned up the corners of her mouth slightly, making

FIG. 133.

FIG. 134.

FIG. 135.

her look more pleasant than the pattern shows. Use the 8-millimeter deep gouge to carve a groove beneath the bottom lip, separating the lips from the chin. Blend the chin upward into this groove. Set in and waste a little more wood from around the jaws if you need to. Draw the eyes on and outline them with a 6-millimeter v-tool. Shape the eyeballs with the knife tip. Carve the eyelids above the eyes, using a tiny (1 or 2-millimeter) v-tool. Draw on the irises. Push a 10-millimeter medium gouge in to outline the irises. Next, draw on the pupils and push a 5-millimeter medium gouge in to outline them. Carve the indentation beneath the nose. Use the 16-millimeter shallow gouge to carve some wood from the sides of the face, making the cheekbones higher. Shape the nose with an 8-millimeter shallow gouge. Carve the nostrils, using a 4-millimeter deep gouge for the inside nostrils, and a 2-millimeter deep gouge to outline the outside nostrils.

FIG. 135. Carve the eyebrows with a 1-millimeter v-tool. Draw on the neck and hair lines which you have cut away. Outline the neck with a 6-millimeter v-tool. Use an 8-millimeter deep gouge to carve a groove under the chin on the neck. This groove is about 5/8 inch deeper than the chin. Carve wood from the neck with the 16-millimeter shallow gouge, blending the neck into the groove which you carved beneath the chin. Fairly long necks look good on female carvings. Be sure to carve this neck as long as the one on the pattern. Set in around the sides of the hair and waste wood away from the background. No wood will be carved away from the tips of the hair as they will blend into the background. An 8-millimeter deep gouge will be used to carve the locks of hair. Go over the locks with a 5-millimeter deep gouge, making some of the cuts deeper and some of the cuts finer, being certain to keep the gouge cuts close together. A female face should be smooth. I have used no sandpaper but have made the cuts smooth by using the chisel. If your cuts are not smooth, you will need to sand this particular carving with fine sandpaper. Finish with shellac and wax.

FIG. 137. Shows the complete piece of driftwood featured in the close up of Fig. 136.

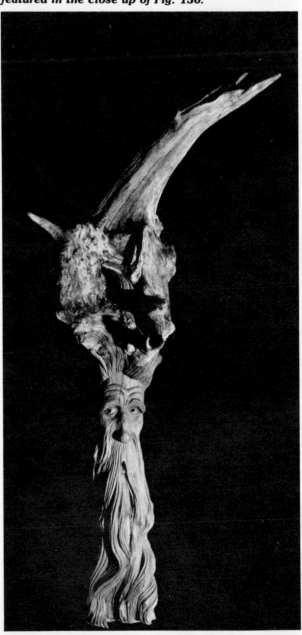

FIG. 136. The remaining figures are examples of driftwood carvings which were carved without using patterns. Close up view of American smokewood carving owned by Ron Raymer.

47

FIG. 138. An Indian carved from walnut driftwood, showing close up of the face and the shape of the complete piece.

FIG. 139. The two top pieces are the same, showing the close up and complete piece which is walnut driftwood. The bottom carving is cedar driftwood.

FIG. 140. Another walnut driftwood carving showing
a close up and the complete piece.

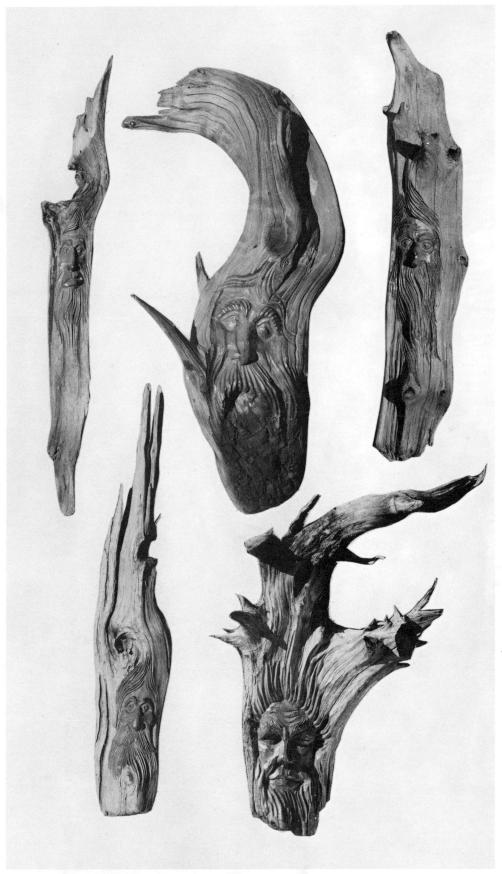

FIG. 141. Various cedar driftwood carvings. The top center carving shows how a charred area may be used to advantage, forming his beard.

FIG. 142. Top carvings are walnut driftwood. Bottom carving is red cedar.

FIG. 143. Center carving was carved from walnut.
Top and bottom carvings are red cedar driftwood.

FIG. 144. Large walnut driftwood carving.